PRAYING WITH THE HOLY SPIRIT

DESTINY IMAGE BOOKS BY COREY RUSSELL

Ancient Paths: Rediscovering Delight in the Word of God

Teach Us to Pray: Prayer that Accesses Heaven and Changes Earth

Reclaiming Revival: Calling a Generation to Contend for Historic Awakening (coauthor: Billy Humphrey)

The Glory Within Study Guide: The Interior Life and the Power of Speaking in Tongues

PRAYING WITH THE HOLY SPIRIT

40 DAYS TO REVOLUTIONIZE YOUR PRAYER LIFE BY ACTIVATING THE GIFT OF TONGUES

COREY RUSSELL

DESTINY IMAGE® PUBLISHERS, INC.

P.O. Box 310, Shippensburg, PA 17257-0310

"Publishing cutting-edge prophetic resources to supernaturally empower the body of Christ"

This book and all other Destiny Image and Destiny Image Fiction books are available at Christian bookstores and distributors worldwide.

For more information on foreign distributors, call 717-532-3040.

Reach us on the Internet: www.destinyimage.com.

ISBN 13 TP: 978-0-7684-7669-9

ISBN 13 eBook: 978-0-7684-7670-5

For Worldwide Distribution, Printed in the U.S.A.

1 2 3 4 5 6 7 8 / 28 27 26 25 24

CONTENTS

A NOTE FROM COREY

I am so excited that you picked up this book. Praying with the Holy Spirit is something that burns within me, and I believe it will transform your life. How can I say that with such certainty? I can say it because praying with the Holy Spirit has radically changed my life. It has opened the Scriptures to me in fresh and dynamic ways. Praying in tongues has also brought me into greater intimacy with what I call the glory within—the wonderful Holy Spirit.

Praying in tongues is not without controversy, however. Some would say that the controversy is reason enough to avoid the subject completely. I strongly disagree. The greatest controversies surround the greatest truths when it comes to important Kingdom realities. Throughout history, controversy and debate have followed doctrines we uphold as absolutely integral today—like the divinity of Christ and the Trinity, for example.

Controversy isn't the only thing that can keep us from taking advantage of the great gift of praying with the Holy Spirit. I can think of a few other reasons for our not speaking in tongues:

- Many of us don't realize just how glorious our salvation really is and what has been made available to us as a result.

- Some of us lack solid, Bible-based teaching on the Holy Spirit and His gifts.
- Many are unaware of all the amazing benefits of praying in the Spirit.
- And then there's the fact that the devil wants to do everything he can to keep us ignorant of the glory within.

The devil does not waste his time on things that do not hurt his kingdom. He knows the power of speaking in tongues, and I am convinced the devil stirs up trouble around the truth of speaking in tongues because he knows the great threat it is to his kingdom. So, don't allow him to keep you from revolutionizing your prayer life by activating the gift of tongues.

My goal is that, by the end of 40 days, you will have a renewed awe of the Person of the Holy Spirit. My prayer is that something will shift in your prayer life over the next few weeks—that you discover how speaking in tongues unlocks the treasure chest of Heaven over your life. It releases supernatural gifts, power, revelation, and understanding. It brings you into precious intimacy with your heavenly Father. May you be stirred afresh to take your place in a generation that gives itself to activating the glorious gift of praying in tongues.

COREY RUSSELL

HOW TO BEST USE THIS BOOK

For this book to have its greatest impact on your life, you will want to give yourself sufficient time and space to take in the readings and pray. You see, we live in a culture where seemingly anything and everything are immediately available to us and right at our fingertips. We don't like the inconvenience of waiting on anything or anybody. But in God's Kingdom, the greatest treasures and pleasures are discovered in the wait. And for a devotional-style book to do its best work in our lives, it requires slowing down and allowing time for thoughtful reading, heart digesting, and Holy Spirit leading.

What you can expect to find in the following pages are 40 devotional readings. These are divided into 8 weeks, each week containing 5 readings. Each day begins with an opening Scripture followed by the devotional reading. And each day closes with a section titled "Tongues Activation Prayer Points." There are 3 prayer points listed for each day. These are there to help you focus on things related to the day's reading and are designed to serve as a launching pad for you simply to converse with Holy Spirit. This is your time to grow in your relationship with the Father through His Holy Spirit.

Each day, you'll want to take this book and your Bible, find a solitary place away from the whirlwinds of life, "shut the door," and fellowship with God through His Holy Spirit. Remember to downshift, take a few deep breaths, welcome the Holy Spirit into your reading, and then begin. Don't rush things. Take time to ponder what you read, inviting Holy Spirit to highlight what the Father is wanting you to see or hear and understand. Pray in the Spirit. Give Him an opportunity to speak to you. Although there are journaling pages included within each day's devotional to write your reflections, feelings and/or reactions, you may want to also have a pen and journal nearby to write what Holy Spirit says to you. That's what will revolutionize you and your prayer life.

WEEK ONE

UNLOCKING THE GLORY OF YOUR SALVATION

Day One

THE GREATEST MIRACLE

To them God willed to make known what are the riches of the glory of this mystery among the Gentiles: which is Christ in you, the hope of glory.
—Colossians 1:27 NKJV

The greatest miracle you could ever receive is the supernatural gift of salvation. This inaugurates a brand-new reality for you: Christ in you. Just let that phrase sink down into your heart right now. "Christ in you." The very Spirit of the Lord Jesus Christ is now living inside you and me, and this Spirit is the hope that we have of the glory to be revealed at Jesus's coming. It doesn't get any higher, any deeper, any wider than this revelation crashing into your life. It's this revelation that was hidden for ages and from generations—but has been revealed in these days to you and me. From the very start, we are going to take our time and reflect on this glorious reality that has become ours. I would even invite you to close your eyes and turn within to behold Jesus.

This glorious reality is greater than any miracle you will ever experience. Greater than blind eyes popping open, deaf ears popping open, and the dead being raised is the Spirit of this Man, Jesus Christ, coming to live inside you. So many of us who have been believers for a long time have the tendency to bypass the most glorious treasure of all. Our awe and understanding of salvation increase when we slow down and go back to what has been done through Christ's death, resurrection, and ascension. This gift of salvation includes far more than we often consider, such as greater power, intimacy with God, and fruit in our lives.

Over the days to come, I am expectant that you are going to come to the realization that the greatest gift you've been looking for is the Person living inside you—waiting to be released through your life. Everything you have desired has already been placed inside you.

TONGUES ACTIVATION PRAYER POINTS

- Thank God for your salvation, for the greatest miracle you have ever received.
- Ask Holy Spirit to rekindle the passion and zeal of first love.
- Ask Him to lead you over the next 40 days into a greater understanding of who He is.

YOUR REFLECTIONS

YOUR REFLECTIONS

Day Two

BEWARE OF FAMILIARITY

When He had come to His own country, He taught them in their synagogue, so that they were astonished and said, "Where did this Man get this wisdom and these mighty works? Is this not the carpenter's son?..."

—Matthew 13:54-55 NKJV

This portion of Scripture is a perfect example of how many of us consider our salvation—as something familiar. The problem is our familiarity has bred corporate powerlessness. In places where Jesus was simply acknowledged as "the carpenter's son," and treated as a young man who was "familiar" to the community, He was actually restrained from accomplishing powerful miracles. Why? Familiarity has the potential to blind us to the power that is right there before our very eyes.

The same principle is applicable for salvation and the indwelling Presence of the Holy Spirit within us. Too many of us have become overly familiar with what is nothing less than the most glorious of realities: God breaking down every barrier to ambush humanity with the intention of making our physical bodies the dwelling place of His Holy Spirit. Such truth is nothing short of astonishing. The problem has been a refusal to take a second look at what we would consider to be the "ABCs" of Christianity. And yet, I believe the very key to unlocking the last-days' release of glory into the earth has everything to do with believers coming into agreement with what they have already received through conversion.

TONGUES ACTIVATION PRAYER POINTS

- Thank Jesus for all that He did to make your salvation possible.
- Ask Holy Spirit to identify areas where familiarity has crept in or where an actual barrier of familiarity exists.
- Ask Him to open your eyes to what Hebrews 2:3 calls "so great a salvation," helping you to see all that has been made available to you in Christ.

YOUR REFLECTIONS

YOUR REFLECTIONS

Day Three

I'M A NEW CREATION

Therefore if any person is [ingrafted] in Christ [the Messiah] he is a new creation [a new creature altogether]; the old [previous moral and spiritual condition] has passed away. Behold, the fresh and new has come!

—2 Corinthians 5:17 AMPC

A new creation with a new nature, a new intimacy with God, a new power over sin, and a new destiny is what happened the moment you and I received Jesus into our lives as our Lord and Savior. What happened in Genesis 1, as great and magnificent as it is, is not as great as what God did when He came to live inside you and me. I love the word *new* because Paul is letting us know that you and I, "in Christ," are something the world has never seen before—new creations.

The moment that Adam sinned, he died a spiritual death. The life of God within him left, and slowly his body followed. Through Christ's death and resurrection and outpouring of the Spirit, that life has now returned, and you and I will never die. Death's sting has been destroyed, and the curse of sin has been broken over us who are "in Him." Though we may die physically, we will be raised again, putting on immortal life, and will live and reign forever with Him.

You are a new creation being prepared for a new heaven and a new earth. What's inside of you right now is reserved for the ages to come. In Revelation 21:5 (NKJV), God Himself said, *"Behold, I make all things new."* This is God's heart and God's purpose, and everything He is doing is about making everything new, and He began with us and our relationship with Him. Today, I want you to lean back, take a deep breath, and begin to repeat the phrase, "I'm a new creation in Christ. The old is gone and the new has come."

TONGUES ACTIVATION PRAYER POINTS

- Thank God for making you a new creation in Christ.
- Ask Holy Spirit to convince you that the old is gone.
- Ask Holy Spirit to remind you throughout the day that you have been made new.

YOUR REFLECTIONS

YOUR REFLECTIONS

DAY FOUR

THE SEED OF GOD LIVES INSIDE YOU

Whoever has been born of God does not sin, for His seed remains in him; and he cannot sin, because he has been born of God.
—1 JOHN 3:9 NKJV

This is one of those intense passages that scare a lot of us; but in my opinion, it is one of the clearest "litmus test" verses over whether or not someone is saved. John is making it clear that whoever has been born of God will never be a successful sinner. I don't know about you, but after I was born again, I tried to do some things that, previously, I did with no regret at all. But doing them after being born again left me feeling like I was falling immediately into hell. The very feelings of regret, conviction, and fear were all signs that I was in fact born of God and that I was a son of God.

If you are struggling with areas of sin and are pained over it to the point of being willing to do something about it, know that you are experiencing the life of God in you. I tell people to fear when they go months and years without any sense of remorse over their current state in God. Again, when we come into Christ, we are a new creation with a new nature and new desires. The person who has been born of God has a harder time being a successful sinner than a cat does barking. The two realities don't go together. Know this—if you are warring against areas of sin in your life, you are loved by God. You are a lover of God who is struggling with sin, not a sinner who is struggling to love God. The difference between those two realities is huge.

The next phrase of this verse is absolutely astounding. God's *"seed remains in him."* The very DNA seed of the eternal God is living in you right now. What this simply means is that in the same way your parents' DNA resides within you and you carry and exemplify similar traits, characteristics, body types, hair color, nose, ears, etc., so it is with God. His DNA lives in you, and as you grow in Him, His life and His character will be formed in and through you, and you will begin to look like His Son.

TONGUES ACTIVATION PRAYER POINTS

- Thank God that you have been born again and His seed remains in you.
- Confess those areas where you are struggling with sin and ask for forgiveness, knowing that God is faithful to forgive and cleanse you.

- Ask Holy Spirit to continue to make you more like Jesus, helping you to remember you are no longer bound to walk or live in sin—you're free in Him.

YOUR REFLECTIONS

YOUR REFLECTIONS

DAY FIVE

BORN AGAIN TO SEE THE KINGDOM

Jesus answered and said to him, "Most assuredly, I say to you, unless one is born again, he cannot see the kingdom of God."
—JOHN 3:3 NKJV

Don't you love Jesus? Nicodemus came to Him at night and through flattery was trying to win Jesus over. Jesus cut through all the politics and flattery, and in essence He said, "You don't have a clue who I am and how to enter My Kingdom unless you are born again." What was it like for this educated ruler of the Pharisees to hear that unless he was born again, he couldn't see or enter the Kingdom of God? Jesus brought this brilliant theologian who prided himself in spiritual matters to a bumbling fool asking questions about having to enter back into his mother's womb to be born again.

There is a natural birth, and then there is a spiritual birth that opens us up to a whole new world, a whole new

Kingdom. When we are born again, we are able to perceive and understand what we were blind to before because we are new people. That conversion process requires great humility and awareness that you're in need of something and Someone outside of yourself.

When we are born again, we see everything differently. We see ourselves differently. We see our value, our worth, and our destiny differently. Eternity becomes the most real thing in the world. We see God differently. He goes from a faraway Person to a relational, very present Person to whom we can turn at any time with any problem. We see other people differently. We love those we could not stand before.

We see God's creation differently. I remember sitting on my swing on my front porch just hours after I experienced salvation. I remember looking at the sky and being undone by how blue the sky was, how green the grass was, and how loud the birds were chirping. It was like I had been dead for 20 years and was suddenly alive. And at that moment it hit me—I'm alive!

TONGUES ACTIVATION PRAYER POINTS

- Thank Holy Spirit for overcoming every obstacle and barrier to bring you into the Kingdom.
- Ask Him to continue to reveal the wondrous realities available to you in His Kingdom.
- Ask Him to help you to see things "differently"—to see things from a Kingdom perspective.

YOUR REFLECTIONS

YOUR REFLECTIONS

Week Two

Rediscovering the Holy Spirit: God Inside You

Day One

YOUR UPGRADE

Nevertheless I tell you the truth. It is to your advantage that I go away; for if I do not go away, the Helper will not come to you; but if I depart, I will send Him to you.
—John 16:7 NKJV

This week, I want us to start looking at the reality of how this hope in glory is experienced. It's obvious that Jesus the Man does not live inside of us, so we have to ask ourselves: What does Christ in me look like? John 13–17 powerfully helps us answer this question, as these are absolutely revolutionary chapters of Scripture when it comes to introducing the Person and purpose of Holy Spirit. I encourage you to take some time and read these five chapters in John, because I want you to recognize the upgrade you have received of Holy Spirit.

Did you know that what you possess inside you is actually an advantage beyond what the disciples experienced, even though they lived in proximity to the Person of Jesus Christ? I have to believe that what Jesus said in John 16:7

was absolutely mind-blowing to them. *How could there be an advantage beyond having You here?* Surely thoughts like this raced through their minds. The reality is, Holy Spirit was contained in the body of one Man while Jesus was on the earth. Because of the Cross and, ultimately, Pentecost, this same Spirit would be released to all who would call upon the name of the Lord, generation after generation, spanning the globe. Are you beginning to see the upgrade you've received in Holy Spirit?

TONGUES ACTIVATION PRAYER POINTS

- Thank Holy Spirit for the upgrade in your relationship with the Father.
- Thank Holy Spirit for depositing His very presence into you.
- Ask Him to help you grasp and access every advantage of this new level of intimacy.

YOUR REFLECTIONS

YOUR REFLECTIONS

DAY TWO

PERSON, FORCE, OR THING?

...but if I depart, I will send Him to you.
—JOHN 16:7 NKJV

You probably have noticed by now that I have frequently referred to the Holy Spirit as simply, "Holy Spirit." From here on out, I want to consistently identify Holy Spirit without a "the" introducing Him. Just as my name is Corey Russell, His name is Holy Spirit. He is not a force field, a fuzzy, or a feeling, He is a Person.

In the same way we don't talk about Jesus as *the Jesus,* we should likewise consider Holy Spirit, as He is equally a Person. This is one of the reasons I am convinced more people do not actually enjoy the advantage of relationship with Holy Spirit. It is easy to have relationship with a Person; it is another thing to try and have relationship with a force or even a power source. We will respond to Holy Spirit based on how we see Him—correctly or incorrectly. If we see Holy

Spirit as some type of force or divine energy, then we will resist engaging Him in relationship as we would the Father or Jesus.

Again, it is easy to have relationship with One identified as the Father or Son, but the *Spirit?* I encourage you to shift the way you view Holy Spirit, for He is just as much God and just as much a Person as the Father and Son. Before your relationship goes to a new level, and you begin to interact with Him differently, it is absolutely key that first and foremost you see and treat Holy Spirit like a Person. I guarantee you, once that perspective shift takes place, your relationship with Him will go to a whole new level.

TONGUES ACTIVATION PRAYER POINTS

- Thank Jesus for the Person of the Holy Spirit.
- Ask Holy Spirit to correct any misconceptions you have about Him.
- Ask Holy Spirit to take your relationship to new levels in the days ahead.

YOUR REFLECTIONS

YOUR REFLECTIONS

DAY THREE

WHAT WILL HE DO?

When He, the Spirit of truth, has come, He will guide you into all truth; for He will not speak on His own authority, but whatever He hears He will speak; and He will tell you things to come. He will glorify Me, for He will take of what is Mine and declare it to you.
—JOHN 16:13-14 NKJV

Jesus tells us that when Holy Spirit comes, He will do several things. He will guide you into all truth. He will not speak on His own authority, and He will speak whatever He hears. He will tell you things to come. He will glorify Jesus. He will take the things that belong to Jesus and declare them to you. What a job description! The clearer we are on who He is, where He lives, and what He does, the clearer our relationship will become.

Holy Spirit's job description is to guide us. He does this by the still small voice within. He does this by highlighting the Word of God. He does this through dreams and visions.

He does this through other people. His desire is to bring you into all truth, and truth is a Person. His name is Jesus.

Holy Spirit is submitted to the Father and the Son and will speak (to those who have ears to hear) whatever He is hearing. I love to ask Holy Spirit, "What are You hearing, Holy Spirit?" Holy Spirit will tell you what's coming. He will do this for you individually. He will tell you what's coming with friends, family, churches, cities, and nations. He is a Prophet, and He will tell you what's coming. His whole aim is glorifying Jesus.

If you will take the time to listen, He will take the things that belong to Jesus and make them known to you. I would encourage you to turn within, focus on the indwelling Holy Spirit, and begin to ask Him to guide you, to speak to you, to open up your understanding. I promise that He will answer you!

TONGUES ACTIVATION PRAYER POINTS

- Thank God for sending you Holy Spirit as your Guide and Teacher.
- Invite Him to lead you into all truth and to open up the Scriptures to you.
- Ask Holy Spirit, "What are You hearing? What is the Father saying?"

YOUR REFLECTIONS

YOUR REFLECTIONS

DAY FOUR

THE PERSON WHO KNOWS GOD BEST

...For the Spirit searches all things, yes, the deep things of God. For what man knows the things of a man except the spirit of the man which is in him? Even so no one knows the things of God except the Spirit of God. Now we have received, not the spirit of the world, but the Spirit who is from God, that we might know the things that have been freely given to us by God.

—1 CORINTHIANS 2:10-12 NKJV

In my opinion, the opening verses provide the clearest job description of Holy Spirit. Paul makes several amazing statements, beginning with the first one: *"The Spirit searches all things."* I love the word search. I don't know about you, but I absolutely love internet *searches*. I love being able to type in a name or a phrase and getting access to hundreds, sometimes thousands, of websites that contain the information connected to that name. And the thing that blows me away is that it's a human-made search engine! What does the search engine of Heaven know of the things of God? What does Holy

Spirit know about Jesus our Bridegroom, God our Father, our King, our Creator? How many verses and thoughts and phrases does Holy Spirit have concerning God Himself?

It's my lifelong pursuit to find out what Holy Spirit knows about God. He searches the deep things of God. What are the "deep things of God"? I have to know, and I won't stop until I find out!

I love that the "deep things" the Holy Spirit searches out concerning God are not for some elite group off in the desert, but are for simple, everyday people like you and me with no special abilities, giftings, or influence. Our inheritance is to know the deep things of God.

Jesus says in Matthew 13:11 that it has been given to us to know the mysteries of the Kingdom. Our inheritance is for Holy Spirit to take the things that belong to God and make them known to you and me. When the Spirit of revelation touches our hearts, nothing can stop us. We love more, give more, believe more, and sacrifice more when those deep things are made known to us. Let's ask Him today for them!

TONGUES ACTIVATION PRAYER POINTS

- Thank Holy Spirit for His surpassing knowledge and understanding about the Kingdom of God.
- Ask Him to reveal the mysteries of the Kingdom.
- Ask Him for your inheritance—to know the deep things of God.

YOUR REFLECTIONS

YOUR REFLECTIONS

DAY FIVE

WHO IS HE SHARING WITH?

But as it is written: "Eye has not seen, nor ear heard, nor have entered into the heart of man the things which God has prepared for those who love Him." But God has revealed them to us through His Spirit....

—1 CORINTHIANS 2:9-10 NKJV

I love these verses. I love that there are things that no eye has ever seen, or no ear has ever heard, or that there are things that have never entered the human heart. That by itself is amazing! But Paul continues and adds a little something to Isaiah's prophecy by saying that none of those things have dawned on the eyes, ears, and hearts of the ones who love God. Do you love God? Well, if you do, then this verse gives you a sneak peak of what eternity will look like. God has eternity to set up billions of years of surprises for you and me. He will be freshly blowing our minds with discoveries of who He is, who we are, what He has done, and what He will do. This is absolutely amazing!

Ephesians 2:7 (NKJV) tells us *"that in the ages to come He might show the exceeding riches of His grace in His kindness toward us in Christ Jesus."* For the next billion years, God will be showing you and me off as the trophies of His grace and kindness in raising us up and seating us with His Son. We will never "get over" the fact that God has sent His Son to the earth to become a Man, live the life we could never live, die our death, and then raise us up with Himself from the dead and seat us together with Himself.

Paul then goes on to say that God has revealed these realities of eternity to us now by the Spirit who lives within us. Beloved, you have the powers of the age living inside you right now. Drink today of eternity and be filled!

TONGUES ACTIVATION PRAYER POINTS

- Thank Holy Spirit for opening up the realm of mystery and sharing the deep things of God with you.
- Tell God how much you look forward to seeing what no eye has seen nor ear has heard in the life to come.
- Ask Holy Spirit to fill you to overflowing.

YOUR REFLECTIONS

YOUR REFLECTIONS

Week Three

Keys to Enjoying Deeper Communion with Holy Spirit

DAY ONE

YOU WERE CREATED FOR DIVINE FELLOWSHIP

Then God said, "Let Us make man in Our image, according to Our likeness...."
—GENESIS 1:26 NKJV

God made you in His image and likeness. He created you for Himself, for deep intimacy and communion. Nothing else in creation was fashioned in such a way. From the animals to the plant life, all other forms of the living created order were not made to where they could actually be compatible with God. This was His intent from the very beginning for man. He created us with internal capacities to relate with God, spirit to Spirit, and with the capacity and ability to represent Him to the rest of the created order.

The very first thing God did after creating Adam was plant a garden. He then put Adam in the garden and gave him the command to tend and cultivate this garden, because this would be the place God would come meet with him and fill him with the knowledge of His will. God's desire through the Old Testament is that He would dwell among us and us with Him. This is what He wants. David caught this vision and gave his life to the fulfillment of it when he cried out, *"I will not give sleep to my eyes or slumber to my eyelids, until I find a place for the Lord, a dwelling place for the Mighty One of Jacob"* (Psalm 132:4-5 NKJV).

When approaching the subject of Holy Spirit, you must settle it: God wants to be as close to you as possible. It's His desire. It's His longing. Jesus prayed in John 17:24 (NKJV), *"Father, I desire that they also whom You gave Me may be with Me where I am."* That's what He wants. That's why He created us. That's why He died, and that's why He's coming again.

TONGUES ACTIVATION PRAYER POINTS

- Thank God for dwelling within you and having sweet communion with you.
- Invite Holy Spirit to come and minister to your heart.
- Tell Him just how much you desire to experience His manifest presence right there where you are.

YOUR REFLECTIONS

YOUR REFLECTIONS

Day Two

AN OLD TESTAMENT SHADOW OF COMMUNION

Do you not know that you are the temple of God and that the Spirit of God dwells in you?
—1 Corinthians 3:16 NKJV

God's dilemma has always been filling a structure that He doesn't destroy when He manifests Himself. Every time God shows up, buildings start shaking, mountains start quaking, heavens start moving because the eternal, infinite God steps down into our little world, and it can barely handle His glory.

When Isaiah saw the Lord in the temple, the posts of the door were shaken. When God showed up on Sinai, no one could even touch the mountain, or they would die. When God designed the human body, He answered this dilemma by creating a structure that could contain His glory and not be destroyed by it. You need to thank God that there isn't smoke coming out of your ears right now or that you actually didn't blow up in your sleep last night! Paul affirms this reality when he told the Corinthians, *"You are the temple of God."* Through the shed blood of Jesus Christ, you have been cleansed and made a suitable dwelling place for His Spirit.

In the Old Testament, we see God relating to man in different ways. We see Him coming to man and being with man; but in the New Testament, we see God *in* man. This is absolutely astounding as we consider that the God of Sinai, the God of the Red Sea, the God of Genesis 1 has made you and me His home through the death, resurrection, and ascension of Jesus Christ. Today, I encourage you to consider the fact that the veil of separation has been removed, and through Holy Spirit, God lives in you right now.

TONGUES ACTIVATION PRAYER POINTS

- Thank Holy Spirit for His abiding presence that has taken up residence in you.
- Tell Him what His dwelling within you, being ever-present with you, means to you.
- Ask Him to address any doubt or fear that could be keeping you from giving Him total access to your heart so that you can have deeper communion with Him.

YOUR REFLECTIONS

YOUR REFLECTIONS

DAY THREE

YOU ARE HOLY SPIRIT'S DWELLING PLACE

...For you are the temple of the living God. As God has said: "I will dwell in them and walk among them. I will be their God, and they shall be My people."
—2 CORINTHIANS 6:16 NKJV

In yesterday's devotional and today's, we see the two different times that Paul calls us the temple of the living God. In each of these verses, the larger context is Paul calling the Corinthians out of sin. I think it's amazing how the apostle Paul reminds these believers that they are the temple of the living God as the motivator to not allow any sin to dwell in them. One of the greatest motivations in my life to live holy is knowing that God has given me His very depth, His very life. When I consider this investment in me, it causes such gratitude and care to protect this at all costs.

Have you ever walked around with a lot of cash in your pockets? How do you walk? I've had lots of cash in my pockets before, and when it's there, I put it all in the front pockets and usually have my hands either on or in my pockets. Why do I do this? Because of the value of money that is on me! What if we cared for the life of God within us in such a way that we were more aware of what we looked at, listened to, talked about, engaged with?

Holy Spirit's first name is Holy, and the more and more that we grow in understanding of who He is and how utterly amazing it is that this Person has made us His home, the greater our desire to guard this relationship at all costs should be. We know from Ephesians 5 that Holy Spirit can be grieved by the way we talk. I've experienced firsthand Holy Spirit being grieved from what I've looked at or what I've listened to; and when this has touched me, I've set my heart to never purposely do anything to harm our relationship.

Today, I want you to turn within and behold that living flame dwelling deep within you and ask Him to reveal any areas that have or could potentially affect your relationship. I've settled it that intimacy and communion with Holy Spirit is the greatest way to live.

TONGUES ACTIVATION PRAYER POINTS

- Thank Holy Spirit for the gift of conviction—for convicting you of sin.
- Confess any sin or shame to Him.
- Ask Him to make you holy as He is holy and help you to become more aware of what you're looking at, listening to, talking about, and engaging with.

YOUR REFLECTIONS

YOUR REFLECTIONS

DAY FOUR

WORD AND SPIRIT: YOU CAN'T HAVE ONE WITHOUT THE OTHER

...The words that I speak to you are spirit, and they are life.

—JOHN 6:63 NKJV

Over the next two days, I want us to focus on one of the key ways that we fellowship with Holy Spirit—meditation on the Word of God. As I have said before, we cannot divorce the Spirit and the Word. The two are one and the same Person, and you cannot have one without the other. As we seek to grow in deeper intimacy with Holy Spirit, know right now that Holy Spirit's favorite chariot to ride in is the Word of God. There is no greater place of Holy Spirit encounter than in long and loving meditation in the Word of God, and there is no greater place of encountering truth than when talking to Holy Spirit. He is called the Spirit of Truth.

Learning how to receive the "Spirit" of Jesus's words is the journey we are on. In John 6, Jesus spoke the "eat

My flesh and drink My blood" teaching (see John 6:54,56 NKJV). This was a very hard teaching and caused many people to turn away and stop following Him because they didn't understand His language. Jesus is making it clear that He is not advocating cannibalism, but He is calling them to feed on His words as their life.

Next week, we are going to begin to shift into the glory and power of speaking in tongues. I've found that the greatest way to enhance my times of praying in tongues is meditating in the Word of God. I've seen many people get weird when they speak in tongues all the time but have no life or depth in the Word of God. I've also seen people who know a lot of Bible verses but are dry as bones because they are not intimate with the Spirit of the Word.

As you read the Word, slow down and quietly repeat phrases back to God that are sticking out to you. Lightly intermingle praying in the Spirit as you read. As phrases increase, write them down and just keep reading. Your life will never be the same!

TONGUES ACTIVATION PRAYER POINTS

- Thank Holy Spirit for setting your heart to receive instruction from Him in the Word of God.
- Ask Him to give you understanding of what you're reading.
- Ask Him to highlight phrases within the Word that will transform your life.

YOUR REFLECTIONS

YOUR REFLECTIONS

DAY FIVE

THE GREATEST BIBLE TEACHER ON THE PLANET

But the anointing which you have received from Him abides in you, and you do not need that anyone teach you....
—1 JOHN 2:27 NKJV

Did you know that there is an anointing that lives inside you? You have received the anointing that teaches you, guides you, and reveals the Word of God to you. No matter how small or ungifted you feel, there is an anointing inside you.

I believe it is important to build on the truth we focused on yesterday, as this is a much-needed area of breakthrough in all our personal walks with Holy Spirit. We *must* start accessing what we have received in the Person of Holy Spirit. He is that wonderful anointing inside us, awaiting communion. In the verse above, the apostle John takes our concept of Bible study to a whole new level when he tells us that the anointing we have received in the Person of Holy Spirit makes it possible to be taught, led, directed, guided, and empowered by the Spirit.

Jesus Himself said that *"the Helper, the Holy Spirit, whom the Father will send in My name, He will teach you all things..."* (John 14:26 NKJV). I am blown away by the phrase *"all things."* Are you struggling in your Bible study time? Is it boring, stale, and dry? Do you feel like you are just reading words on a page and doing your best to get through to the next chapter? I encourage you, invite Holy Spirit into the process. The anointing He gives shines a supernatural light on Scripture, opening your eyes to new understanding as you actually study the Bible with Holy Spirit.

I've written a book titled *Ancient Paths: Rediscovering Delight in the Word of God.* In this book, I talk about ways to move out of boredom into a place of delight in the Word of God. As you read, slow down, and as verses touch you, turn them into prayers back to God. Lightly intermingle praying in the Spirit and short prayers. He will help you and teach you as you go. The Word of God is starting a conversation. It's more than a duty or discipline. It's a conversation with the Person of God.

TONGUES ACTIVATION PRAYER POINTS

- Thank God for His Word.
- Invite Holy Spirit to take your study of His Word to the next level.
- Ask Him to unveil Jesus—the Word—to you in greater ways than what you could experience in your own strength with your own intellect.

YOUR REFLECTIONS

YOUR REFLECTIONS

Week Four

The Importance of Speaking in Tongues

Day One

IT'S LEGAL TO DESIRE SPIRITUAL GIFTS

...earnestly desire and cultivate the spiritual endowments [gifts]....
—1 Corinthians 14:1 AMPC

The first three weeks were dedicated to establishing a foundation to build on. We've looked at the glorious reality of our salvation, the identity of the One who lives inside of us, and some of the ways to fellowship with Holy Spirit.

Now, I want to focus on the key catalyst for communion that we will be discussing throughout the rest of this book—tongues. The first thing I want to do now is completely clear the air and invite you into a wholehearted pursuit of the fullness of God being experienced and released in your life. As we will learn, the apostle Paul knew something about spiritual gifts, and particularly speaking in tongues. He was not ashamed of it, but on the contrary, he invited all believers to *earnestly desire and cultivate* these realities in our lives.

I'm coming to realize that the very thing that the Charismatic church is known for—speaking in tongues—is the very practice it engages the least. Many have received a touch from Holy Spirit, been baptized in the Spirit, spoke in tongues, and then memorialized the experience. We treat it like our spiritual badge. "I got that," or "I had that happen to me," or "I spoke in tongues." Whether we spoke in tongues has little meaning when it comes to today. I want to stir you to not only return to the place of praying in tongues, but I want to give you a vision for extended times of praying in tongues.

Many of us have reduced this experience to falling down at the altar with these languages coming out of us, but I want to give you a vision for praying in tongues when you wake up, when you are driving to school or work, when you are doing the dishes, when you are at the grocery store, and in many other ways and places.

In this way, you as the temple of God are living a life of unceasing prayer. This should not be considered taboo, back-room stuff. Paul spent a great deal of time focusing on this practice of believers praying in a personal prayer language. Why? Little keys open big doors. I believe praying in tongues is a gateway to the other gifts of the Spirit, the fruit of the Spirit, and the power of the Spirit.

TONGUES ACTIVATION PRAYER POINTS

- Thank Holy Spirit for the spiritual gifts He has given you.

- Express to Him that you want everything He has for you.
- Ask Holy Spirit to help you cultivate those gifts, including the gift of tongues.

YOUR REFLECTIONS

YOUR REFLECTIONS

Day Two

A GLIMPSE INTO APOSTLE PAUL'S DEVOTIONAL LIFE

I thank God that I speak in tongues more than any of you.

—1 Corinthians 14:18 NLT

When it comes to forerunners in the faith who have blazed trails and accomplished mighty exploits for the Kingdom, the apostle Paul stands out above the rest. The very man who wrote the majority of the New Testament and helped spread the gospel across the known world says that he spoke in tongues more than the rest of the Corinthian church. This is amazing!

I've asked myself the question many times: How could the busiest, most effective, most powerful apostle make such a bold statement to the Corinthian church? How could the man who exemplified the character of Christ, the love of Christ, and the power of Christ say such a bold statement?

Here is, in my opinion, the clearest window into his personal devotional life. This was a man who was undeniably sold out to the Holy Spirit and grateful for His gifts, and I believe his example invites us to make a decision. Paul's example refuses to let us remain "on the fence" about praying in tongues.

The Message version phrases 1 Corinthians 14:18 this way, *"I'm grateful to God for the gift of praying in tongues that he gives us for praising him, which leads to wonderful intimacies we enjoy with him. I enter into this as much or more than any of you."* I pray these words are even now awakening you to know and experience God in the way that Paul did. Could it be that the "secret" to intimacy and power that you've been looking for is found in that gift you received years ago, but have not really engaged with?

I'm convinced that as we begin to give ourselves to extended times of praying in tongues, we will see the destinies and breakthroughs that we've been looking for start to come forth. Paul's experience was not isolated and restricted only to him—a "super apostle." He modeled something accessible and available to each one of us today; otherwise, he would not have shared such detailed instruction on it.

If Paul was grateful for the gift of praying in tongues, I propose that it is something we need to pursue in our own lives. It's something that we need to develop, and it's a lost reality that we need to steward well. If you have not received it yet, we are moving in that direction. Get ready! If you have received it, I invite you to rekindle the fire and draw from that glorious river within.

TONGUES ACTIVATION PRAYER POINTS

- Thank God for giving you the gift of speaking in tongues.
- Tell Holy Spirit how much you desire to walk with God like the apostle Paul, powerfully enriched by praying in tongues.
- Ask Him to rekindle the fire so that you can draw from that glorious river within.

YOUR REFLECTIONS

YOUR REFLECTIONS

DAY THREE

TONGUES REVEAL THE HUMILITY AND WISDOM OF GOD

Assuredly, I say to you, unless you are converted and become as little children, you will by no means enter the kingdom of heaven.

—MATTHEW 18:3 NKJV

God's Kingdom is based on humility. The only way we enter His Kingdom and, in turn, abide in His Kingdom is through humility. Scripture tells us that God purposefully chooses weak, insignificant things to manifest His power through. And so it is with the glorious reality of speaking in tongues. It blows me away that God chooses to hide His most glorious realities in common, mundane, ugly, even offensive ways. Let's consider a few.

To start, the coming of Jesus the Messiah—in a dirty, smelly stable in Bethlehem. The King of kings born like a pauper. Likewise, consider His death. He actually establishes

His Kingdom by laying down His life. To the natural mind and human wisdom, it makes little sense.

But then again, it's truly the glory of God to hide a matter, and our glory to seek it out. Wise men sought His glory, journeying from a long distance to embrace the wisdom of God manifested in a manger. Just as the Messiah was birthed in humble conditions, God births His Church through a bunch of untrained fishermen, acting drunk, speaking in other tongues.

I propose to you that before we specifically wrestle with speaking in tongues, we need to discover what we really believe about God, His wisdom, and His ways, as tongues is just one expression of how His Kingdom is released. It's amazing how God's mysteries are revealed through babblings.

This is why tongues are so offensive to many people. It is a direct affront to our minds and to our natural reasoning. We will continue to stumble over Kingdom realities until we humble ourselves and embrace God's wisdom. This makes me think of the game of limbo—how low can you go?

In Matthew 18, Jesus wasn't just speaking of a spiritual conversion where we get saved. Our minds need to become converted as well. We need to embrace Kingdom paradigms. Yes, the Kingdom is one of success, victory, and power, but how we access these realities is through getting low. Our level of humility gauges what we experience and release of God's supernatural power.

Worship leader Laura Hackett wrote a song about how God's river rushes to low places. This is absolutely true. We must humble ourselves to God's wisdom and methods, completely surrendering to His way of doing things.

TONGUES ACTIVATION PRAYER POINTS

- Thank Jesus for His example of humility.
- Surrender your heart and life anew and afresh to the Father.
- Ask Holy Spirit to help you walk in humility and obedience before the Father, even when what He wants you to do doesn't compute with your natural way of thinking.

YOUR REFLECTIONS

YOUR REFLECTIONS

Day Four

UNDERSTANDING THE DIFFERENT EXPRESSIONS OF TONGUES

Then there appeared to them divided tongues, as of fire, and one sat upon each of them. And they were all filled with the Holy Spirit and began to speak with other tongues, as the Spirit gave them utterance.

—Acts 2:3-4 NKJV

Can you imagine what that sound of mighty rushing wind was like? How about seeing divided tongues of fire resting over each one's head? After ten days in an upper room, obeying Jesus's command to tarry in the city, the Promise of the Father was released on the day of Pentecost, and all of history has been changed from that day forward.

What so shocks me is that at the center of this historic moment, God placed the tongues of all the nations on these disciples, and they began to speak in these languages supernaturally, while everyone who was there heard these fishermen speaking their language! Jesus told us this would happen in Mark 16:17 (NKJV): *"And these signs will follow those who believe: In My name they will cast out demons; they will speak with new tongues."*

Tongues are a sign that follows believers. Special believers? Apostles? Super spiritual people? No. It is a sign that follows believers. Period. If you are a believer, you are a prime candidate to receive and, in turn, exercise the gift of tongues.

The New Testament describes three different expressions of speaking in tongues:

1) There is the spiritual gift of delivering a message in tongues, which is accompanied by an interpretation. This is the prophetic expression of tongues Paul is describing in 1 Corinthians 12;

2) There is an evangelistic expression of tongues, where someone shares a message in a known tongue, but it is unknown to and unlearned by the person speaking. We read about this in Acts 2:3-4 as this manifestation of tongues had the disciples speaking in different known languages; and

3) There is the personal, devotional act of praying in tongues. I want you to know right

now that through the glorious gift of speaking in tongues, you can talk straight to your Father in Heaven.

TONGUES ACTIVATION PRAYER POINTS

- Thank God for the outpouring of Holy Spirit on the day of Pentecost.
- Ask Holy Spirit for increased wisdom and understanding about how the gift of tongues is released.
- Ask Him to stir your heart to pursue the gift in greater measure than ever before.

YOUR REFLECTIONS

YOUR REFLECTIONS

Day Five

PREPARE FOR A FRESH FILLING

And do not get drunk with wine, for that is debauchery; but ever be filled and stimulated with the [Holy] Spirit. Speak out to one another in psalms and hymns and spiritual songs, offering praise with voices [and instruments] and making melody with all your heart to the Lord.

—Ephesians 5:18-19 AMPC

Everybody gets drunk on something. This is exactly what Paul is talking about in Ephesians 5:18. Drunk is being underneath the control of something. Paul is making the point: Whose control will you be underneath? God's or the world's? How we satisfy this craving to be filled or under the influence can often be wrong, but the desire in and of itself was wired into us by God Himself. We were made to be filled with something—continually.

God desired and created us to thirst. He made us a thirsty people, and that thirst will be quenched by *something.* The ultimate fulfillment of that thirst is satisfied in the Person of

Holy Spirit. It is an ongoing, ever-increasing reality that we must pursue throughout our lives.

Holy Spirit is not some badge of honor we wear to broadcast our level of spirituality. It does not matter what you encountered 5, 10, 20 years ago at youth camp or during a revival service. Is the river of God flowing fresh in your life today? If not, I want to invite you to come and drink deep.

In Ephesians 5, Paul is literally talking about a continuous lifestyle of being *filled* with the Holy Spirit. The Amplified version is most accurate when capturing the original Greek. It would be like saying, "Be *being* filled with the Spirit." It is not a one-time, fall on the floor, speak in tongues for a season and then on to the next thing type of experience.

As we begin to make room for Holy Spirit to fill us, we can take some practical steps. Paul gives us one of these as he refers to *speaking out to one another* through spiritual songs. When we sing the Word of God and sing in tongues, we are taking some practical steps toward living a life continually filled with Holy Spirit.

As we are filled, we will then begin to see breakthroughs in our lives; the Word of God will come alive like never before; and we will enjoy greater demonstrations of God's presence, power, and character made manifest.

TONGUES ACTIVATION PRAYER POINTS

- Thank Holy Spirit for His desire to refresh you.

- Invite Holy Spirit to fill you to overflowing.
- Ask Him to help you walk daily, continually filled with Him, speaking in tongues, and praying in Him.

YOUR REFLECTIONS

YOUR REFLECTIONS

WEEK FIVE

BENEFITS OF PRAYING IN THE SPIRIT: HOW TO UNLOCK THE REVELATORY REALM OF HEAVEN OVER YOUR LIFE

DAY ONE

WHO ARE YOU REALLY TALKING TO?

For he who speaks in a tongue does not speak to men but to God....
—1 CORINTHIANS 14:2 NKJV

This week, I want us to look at several benefits that come from praying in Holy Spirit. Perhaps the most powerful, if not the most instrumental, is the fact that, by praying in the Spirit, we are talking directly to God. This takes our understanding of intimacy with Him to a whole other dimension.

Keep in mind, while praying in tongues, you are not communicating with people, nor are you talking with demons. You are speaking directly to the Father. This is very important to understand as some mistakenly believe that, by opening themselves up to praying in the Spirit, they are thereby opening a gateway to the demonic realm in their lives. This is a great lie of the deceiver, for the last thing the enemy wants you doing is enjoying spirit-to-Spirit fellowship with God.

The devil is well aware of the benefits that come from such fellowship. In fact, later on, we will discover how praying in the Spirit is actually an offensive weapon when it comes to donning the armor of God and engaging in *offensive* spiritual warfare.

Beloved, you can be confident that when you are praying in another tongue, your spirit is speaking directly to God. No hindrances. No obstructions. No barriers. You and God are in communication as you pray in Holy Spirit. What a blessing and incredible benefit.

When we pray in tongues, we are exchanging intimacies with the Creator of the Universe. *Absolutely incredible!* This truth has so stabilized my prayer life because, in prayer, my mind wanders every five seconds. Reminding myself that I'm talking to God has increased my times of connection with Him.

One of the things that I love to do is to have focal points of God when I pray. I love to picture God on the throne as described in Revelation 4 and God in my spirit as described in Colossians 1:27. Whenever my mind wanders, instead of getting beat up by that fact, I just simply bring my mind back to the focal point and continue to fellowship with God.

Hardly anyone has any access to any president, king, or leader, but through the blood of Jesus and Holy Spirit, you and I have direct access to President of the Universe!

TONGUES ACTIVATION PRAYER POINTS

- Thank Holy Spirit for making a way for you to have direct, intimate connection with the Father.
- Ask Him to help you focus on God on His throne and in your spirit as you pray.
- Ask Him to speak to your heart and help you know it's His voice and not another's.

YOUR REFLECTIONS

YOUR REFLECTIONS

DAY TWO

DEALING WITH THE DISTRACTIONS

For if I pray in a tongue, my spirit prays, but my understanding is unfruitful.
—1 CORINTHIANS 14:14 NKJV

Distractions become a normal part of life when we give ourselves to extended times of praying in tongues. I want to address this subject openly and authentically, as I believe so many people have given up on this gift because of these hindrances and distractions.

In the following days, I give you some practical tools to help you persevere and remain focused. The key to developing praying in tongues as a normal part of life is pressing through the distractions. We cannot give up. In fact, I recommend giving it six months to a year, long term. Remember, this is all about developing a lifestyle that makes room for extended times of praying in tongues. This is not religious obligation—this is a supernatural gift that produces so many benefits in our lives.

Let me share something with you that I have found about praying in tongues. After 20 minutes of praying in tongues, things start to shift. I've noticed over more than 20 years of doing this that my mind begins to clear, the Word of God begins to open, divine thoughts come, I begin to feel what Holy Spirit is feeling, and I receive new prayers and experience a wonderful sense of connection and centering in on the life of God. This doesn't happen 100 percent of the time, but it happens many, many times, and I've come to expect it.

Tomorrow, I share two focal points that have helped me rein in my mind while praying. In the meantime, I want you to understand that praying in the Spirit represents a shift in how we are accustomed to praying, and I believe one of the most important things that takes place is a major transition in maturity. We truly discover what it means to press in and press past. We press into God, pressing past the distractions that try to get us off course.

I've learned through praying in tongues for these times to train my mind and emotions and bring them into divine alignment. I tell people all the time that, if I prayed or specifically prayed in tongues when I felt like it, then I would pray once a month. It's an act of obedience that brings about change. We must move from "feeling like it."

Many times our circumstances, emotions, thoughts, and bodies can keep us from praying, but we must settle that, although the pull away from prayer may still be there, our spirits will arise and run the day.

TONGUES ACTIVATION PRAYER POINTS

- Thank Holy Spirit for being your Guide in prayer.
- Tell Him you trust His leadership and you don't want to lean on your own understanding.
- Ask Him to help you persevere through distractions and interruptions.

YOUR REFLECTIONS

YOUR REFLECTIONS

FOCAL POINT I: GOD ON THE THRONE

Immediately I was in the Spirit; and behold, a throne set in heaven, and One sat on the throne.
—REVELATION 4:2 NKJV

Over the next two days, I am going to describe two focal points that serve as anchors while I pray in tongues. These are images that I focus on to keep my mind grounded and free from distractions.

As I pray in tongues, there are two places that I focus my attention—upward and inward. Today, I want to discuss the upward focus where I fix my gaze upon the scene described in Revelation 4—God on the throne. This is the first place that Jesus took His disciples when giving them a model prayer. He directed them toward their Father in Heaven.

We cannot make this some "out there" reality. What's currently happening in Heaven is very real and very relevant. We must become connected with the culture and environment of Heaven's throne room because even though we are here on earth, our spirit has a place of residence in heavenly places, as Paul describes in Ephesians 2:6. We are on earth but are also privileged to gaze upon the glorious throne room realities of Heaven.

While praying in tongues, I try to focus on what's taking place in Heaven, right now, and actually enter this glorious sanctuary and join the symphony of worship.

Close your eyes and begin praying in tongues. Remember, this throne room encounter was not just limited to John. It was not just his experience—it is your inheritance in Christ. There's an open door for you to enter and "come up" to participate in this majestic scene.

Look upon the One on the throne. Visualize His beauty like jasper. Take your place as one standing upon the sea of glass. Hear the thunderings. See the lightning. I encourage you to read Revelation 4 in your Bible over and over, as it becomes a clearer picture for your mind to gaze upon while praying in tongues.

TONGUES ACTIVATION PRAYER POINTS

- Thank Jesus for making a way for you to approach the throne room of God.
- Ask Holy Spirit to help you picture the heavenly reality of Revelation 4.
- Ask Him to enable you to see God on the throne.

YOUR REFLECTIONS

YOUR REFLECTIONS

DAY FOUR

FOCAL POINT 2: GOD IN YOUR SPIRIT

...Christ in you, the hope of glory.
—COLOSSIANS 1:27 NKJV

The Creator of Heaven and earth lives inside you! The God of all glory lives within your spirit. His power, His presence, His resources, His life—His glory lives inside us. As we move to our second focal point, we are invited to turn within and start accessing this glory.

In the same way that I like to focus on God on the throne, I also focus on God in my spirit. This is the second focal point that I encourage you to have while praying in tongues. Here, you are setting your eyes on the burning fire of God living inside you.

One of the best things you can do with this focal point is look in wonder and awe and to provoke yourself with these questions: Did you know that the Shekinah glory of God lives inside you? How is it possible that the God of Genesis 1:1—who could not be contained by any earthly structure—made a decision to dwell inside you, and your physical frame remains *intact?* Questions like these are a doorway into revelation, as Holy Spirit is the One who will come and start releasing supernatural answers and insight.

One of the clearest pictures of this focal point in action is found in 2 Corinthians 3. Starting in verse 7, Paul blows our minds as he compares the glory of the Old Covenant to what we have received through the Spirit. I feel like Paul is calling us to start tapping into the glorious inheritance that lives inside, and the way he does this is by giving us a focal point to "behold." Verse 18 is key, as Paul notes that "*we all, with unveiled face, beholding as in a mirror the glory of the Lord, are being transformed into the same image from glory to glory, just as by the Spirit of the Lord*" (2 Corinthians 3:18 NKJV).

I encourage you to take time and slow down today. Focus on Holy Spirit living inside you. Set your mind on Him. When you wander, come back to Him. The Man Christ Jesus lives in you by Holy Spirit, and by *beholding* Him, you are being transformed *into His image.*

TONGUES ACTIVATION PRAYER POINTS

- Thank Holy Spirit for His presence within—the glory within.
- Tell Him you want to behold Jesus and be transformed into His image.
- Ask Holy Spirit to give you revelation and understanding of what it is to have Him resident within you.

YOUR REFLECTIONS

YOUR REFLECTIONS

DAY FIVE

UNLOCK THE SPIRIT OF REVELATION

For one who speaks in an [unknown] tongue speaks not to men but to God, for no one understands or catches his meaning, because in the [Holy] Spirit he utters secret truths and hidden things [not obvious to the understanding].

—1 CORINTHIANS 14:2 AMPC

Paul makes an amazing statement here—when we speak in tongues, we are speaking secret truths and hidden things. Other translations call them mysteries (NKJV). These mysteries are not hidden from us, but hidden for us. Tongues are a supernatural way for us to access these mysteries, discover what God is saying, and experience the spirit of revelation in our lives. Remember—in God's Kingdom, hunger is a key currency. The mysteries, secrets, and hidden truths of Heaven are hidden for the hungry. They are reserved for those who desire for and thirst after God. These are truths about God, us, our destinies, and about the plans and purposes of His heart.

Think about with whom you share secrets and hidden truth. The deep plans and purposes of your heart are not for public display—they are reserved for those you are most intimate with, right? God is the same way. The great invitation is that all of us have the ability to be intimate with Him and discover His mysteries.

Matthew 13:11 (NKJV) makes it clear, as Jesus says, *"It has been given to you to know the mysteries of the kingdom of heaven...."* There's but one question: Who will humble themselves to embrace the wisdom and ways of God when it comes to unlocking His mysteries?

When I pray in tongues, divine revelation starts flowing out of God's realm and into me. In essence, I am building a "landing strip" for the spirit of revelation. I'm praying, "Holy Spirit, come land here—in my spirit—with the Word of God." This can happen in many ways.

When we give ourselves to praying in the Spirit for extended periods of time, we begin to access the spirit of revelation in different ways. The still small voice of Holy Spirit gets clearer and clearer; our confidence in hearing God's voice increases; our dream life increases; visions become more prevalent; we become open to receiving words of knowledge, wisdom, and prophecy; and finally, God begins to speak to us about people in need.

In fact, I believe Holy Spirit will begin to show you strategic people to pray for, give you names and specific instructions on how to pray for them, and even set up situations to where you will bump into those people who need ministry, and you will have a *due season* word for them.

TONGUES ACTIVATION PRAYER POINTS

- Thank Holy Spirit for granting you the spirit of revelation.
- Invite Holy Spirit to "land" in your spirit with the Word of God.
- Ask Him to help you hear His voice, to hear the names of people around you whom He wants you to pray for and what it is He may have you say to them.

YOUR REFLECTIONS

YOUR REFLECTIONS

WEEK SIX

BENEFITS OF PRAYING IN THE SPIRIT: KEYS TO BUILDING UP YOUR INNER SELF

Day One

THE IMPORTANCE OF YOUR INTERIOR LIFE

...God judges persons differently than humans do. Men and women look at the face; God looks into the heart.
—1 Samuel 16:7 MSG

Worship leader Misty Edwards wrote a song describing where our real lives actually unfold—behind the face. This is the interior life. In this day and age, we have become absolutely consumed with externals. We are a generation that defines success by "how big" and "how much" and "how many"—but God defines success in a completely different way. The body of Christ is no exception. We can become guilty of focusing so much on the size of our influence over the size of our hearts that we end up losing both.

Looking at our opening verse, when God made this statement to Samuel, He was making it clear that Heaven is looking at our hearts, and that is what we are defined by. What did God see in this young shepherd boy? He saw a future king who was just as content before God and some sheep as he was leading the whole nation of Israel as king. His reward was God.

In the same way that God trained David on the back sides of the hills of Bethlehem, so I believe God is training a generation in this hour that will get lost before the "audience of One." And in the same way that this young man came to the forefront to take on and kill Goliath, so God is going to bring forth a generation that has built up their interior lives, experienced breakthroughs in their souls, and become positioned to step into places of leadership in the coming days to take on the end-time Goliaths.

How does all of this connect to praying in tongues? I'm glad you asked! Praying in tongues is one of the most powerful and practical ways we can build our interior lives. When praying in tongues, we are connecting with the only "eyes" in the world that matter—God's.

Also, we are removing all the debris in our souls that hinder the life of God from flowing in and through us. As the coming rains of glory and crises come, we will be able to stand and navigate through them instead of being destroyed because we have invested in building what is more important.

TONGUES ACTIVATION PRAYER POINTS

- Thank God that He sees and knows you the most and the best.
- Invite Holy Spirit to search your heart and deal with anything He brings to mind that

may be in the way of clear communion and fellowship.

- Ask Him to help you live from the inside out, leading you in the way everlasting.

YOUR REFLECTIONS

YOUR REFLECTIONS

Day Two

YOU ARE GOD'S BUILDING PROJECT

...You are God's building.
—1 Corinthians 3:9 NLT

Just imagine the high price that is paid by those who do not give a natural building a solid foundation. Be it a house or skyscraper—it could be the most beautiful, eye-pleasing structure on the planet. However, appearance won't make any difference when the elements come and threaten the actual stability of the building. Let me put it this way. A building can be thousands of feet wide, but only inches deep. Depth is everything when it comes to developing sturdy foundations, and ultimately, establishing a structure that will be unshakable when the elements come.

I believe the Lord is delivering many of us from focusing primarily on the width or the "reach" of our lives and is focusing us in on the depth of our lives to be able to weather the coming days.

Paul says in 1 Corinthians 14:4 that when we pray in tongues, we *"edify"* ourselves. That word *edify* comes from the same Latin root as *edifice*, which means a "massive, magnificent building." As we pray for extended times in tongues, we are erecting, strengthening, and solidifying the building called our interior life to house and steward the life of God within us.

In the same way you need to insert your computer charger into a source of electricity to receive power for your computer, so it is with praying in tongues. When we pray in tongues, we are plugging our interior life into the power of the indwelling Holy Spirit.

I love all of the different things that I receive from other people, but I can edify myself. I can strengthen myself in God. Jude 1:20 (NKJV) calls it *"building yourselves up on your most holy faith, praying in the Holy Spirit."* I'm convinced that, if you will begin to set apart 25 minutes every day to focus on God and pray in the Holy Spirit, you will see the Master Builder go to work—even at an accelerated pace—in your life. Try it. *I dare you!*

TONGUES ACTIVATION PRAYER POINTS

- Thank Holy Spirit for building the very life of God inside you.
- Share with Holy Spirit your desire to have a powerful and intimate devotional life with the Father.
- Ask Him to continue to make you "God's building" with greater depth and a richer relationship.

YOUR REFLECTIONS

YOUR REFLECTIONS

DAY THREE

EDIFYING YOURSELF

He who speaks in a tongue edifies himself....
—1 CORINTHIANS 14:4 NKJV

We are living in a day when personal fitness and health is becoming more and more common. I love it and am seeking to embrace it in my life as well as in my family. But at the same time, I'm convinced that if we were as focused on the current state of our interior lives as we are our exterior lives, we would see an explosion of revival break out all over the Church. There are many believers who look like Arnold Schwarzenegger on the outside and yet look like Minnie Mouse on the inside.

The number-one result that produces strength when working out is resistance—the resistance of the weight produces strength and tone. It's the same way with praying in tongues. You will find out quickly, as you launch into a journey of extended times of praying in tongues, the resistance you will face within your own soul. The pull of human nature is toward complacency, apathy, and laziness; and it's through praying in tongues that we "swim against the current" of our emotions and feelings. It's in this place where we become mighty in spirit!

John the Baptist was in the wilderness and "he became strong in spirit." He didn't become strong in personality, charisma, or even gifting—he became strong in spirit. Becoming mighty in spirit is, in my opinion, the greatest need of the hour.

In Ephesians 3:16 (NLT), Paul prayed that God will *"empower you with inner strength through his Spirit"*; and in Colossians 1:11 (NLT), he prayed that we *"will be strengthened with all his glorious power."* Paul understood that interior might is what we need to walk out a Christian life filled with joy and peace through every season of life.

I'm convinced that the power of praying in tongues for extended periods of time has connected my inner self to the riches of *His* power and glory that reside within me. As I break through all my changing emotions and wandering thoughts, accessing the light and power of God within me, I'm strengthened from the inside out, and it radically changes my thought life, emotional chemistry, and desires.

TONGUES ACTIVATION PRAYER POINTS

- Thank Holy Spirit for strengthening and building up your inner self as you pray in tongues.
- Ask Him to empower you to break through apathy and complacency in your prayer life.
- Ask Him to strengthen and equip you "according to His glorious power."

YOUR REFLECTIONS

YOUR REFLECTIONS

DAY FOUR

YOU ARE LED BY THE SPIRIT

For as many as are led by the Spirit of God are children of God.
—ROMANS 8:14 NLT

God has designed us intentionally—body, soul, and spirit. Just as the tabernacle contained the outer court, the inner court, and the Holy of Holies, so God has built us in the same way. Our bodies are the outer court, our souls (mind, will, and emotions) are the inner court, and our spirits are the Holy of Holies.

The day you are born again, the very glory of God takes up residence within your spirit. That which was once dead is now alive by the Spirit of God. God has designed you in such a way that the reality within your spirit would transform the reality in your soul and body.

As we spend extended times praying in tongues, the life of God in our spirits coupled with the Word of God begins to spring up, changing over time our thought lives, emotional chemistry, desires, and even our physical bodies. Paul states in Romans 8:11 (NKJV) that *"the Spirit of Him who raised Jesus from the dead dwells in you, He who raised Christ from the dead will also give life to your mortal bodies through His Spirit who dwells in you."* It's amazing that the resurrection power of God resides in me and has the potential to give life and power to my physical body.

Paul states a few verses later that *"as many as are led by the Spirit of God, these are sons of God"* (Romans 8:14 NKJV). Think about what it means to be *"led by the Spirit."* You can also put in the word *governed* or *under the leadership.* Many times, I'm more led by my soul than I am by my spirit. The circumstances that come my way throw my thought life and emotions into a swirl, and I lose my way.

When we pray in tongues, we are in essence telling our souls to get into the backseat and our spirits to get into the driver's seat. My desire is that my spirit would lead the way. This doesn't mean that bad circumstances and situations won't come my way. What it does mean is that I can have divine perspective in the middle of the storms of life. *Perspective is everything.*

TONGUES ACTIVATION PRAYER POINTS

- Thank Holy Spirit for His being with you and in you.
- Ask Him to continue to lead you, to go before you and with you.
- Ask Him to increase your sensitivity to His voice as you pray with Him.

YOUR REFLECTIONS

YOUR REFLECTIONS

DAY FIVE

PREPARING A HIGHWAY FOR HIS GLORY

...Prepare the way of the Lord; make straight in the desert a highway for our God. Every valley shall be exalted and every mountain and hill brought low; the crooked places shall be made straight and the rough places smooth; the glory of the Lord shall be revealed, and all flesh shall see it together....

—ISAIAH 40:3-5 NKJV

In the same way that God raised up John the Baptist to "go before" the first coming of Jesus, God is raising up forerunners all around the earth who are being called forth to prepare the earth for the second coming of Jesus. Before they come forth to prepare this highway on earth, they must first learn how to cooperate with Holy Spirit in the preparation of the highway within their own hearts.

Can you imagine all the demolition and clearing that is involved in building a highway? I remember a highway being built near my hometown when I was growing up, and when the highway route approached a huge mountain, the only thing the builders could do to make a way through the mountain was to use dynamite to clear it out. This is literally the picture I get when giving myself to extended times of praying in tongues. I'm seeking to see the glory within released into my thought life, emotional chemistry, and body, but it must demolish, destroy, and remove existing strongholds, arguments, and emotions that exalt themselves against the knowledge of God.

One of the greatest realities that I believe praying in tongues has taught me is cultivating the "breaker anointing" in my life. When those times of resistance rise up within me, I lean in knowing that God is the God of the breakthrough, and that small breakthroughs today are training me for big breakthroughs tomorrow.

Through praying in tongues and the Word of God, you will begin to see the valleys of shame and guilt raised up. You will begin to see the mountains of pride and independence brought low. You will begin to see the crooked places of distortion straightened, and all the rough places of religion and harshness made smooth.

Why is all this happening? So that the glory of the Lord would be revealed in us and through us. This is our inheritance.

TONGUES ACTIVATION PRAYER POINTS

- Thank Holy Spirit for preparing the way of the Lord in your heart and life.

- Ask Him to continue to enlarge your capacity to carry and release His presence.
- Acknowledge He is Lord of your spirit and ask Him to reign over every area of your life.

YOUR REFLECTIONS

YOUR REFLECTIONS

Week Seven

Waging Victorious Spiritual Warfare

DAY ONE

ENLISTED FOR WARFARE

Fight the good fight of faith....
—1 TIMOTHY 6:12 NKJV

This week, we are going to look at the power of tongues as it pertains to the call to daily warfare against the schemes of the devil from within and without. We are called to war, not from a place of trying to accomplish victory, but from a place of standing on the victory of the finished work of the Cross. Through Jesus's death and resurrection, the powers of hell were disarmed, and the keys of hell were taken. We who were once dead were set free from sin and death and raised up with Him and seated together with Him in the heavenly places to join Him and execute the finished work.

Many believers will just conclude that Jesus did everything for them, so they don't have to do anything, yet Paul repeated many times in the Epistles to believers that they must "fight" and "wage the good warfare." First Peter 5:8 states that the devil walks about like a roaring lion, seeking whom he may devour. Our response to this is not to become fearful, but to be sober, aware, and not ignorant of the enemy's schemes.

God has given us two massive weapons in this war—the *Word of God* coupled with *praying in Holy Spirit.* These two weapons, when used, bring change to the greatest place of warfare—our minds. As we pray in tongues and declare the Word of God, strongholds and arguments are dethroned in our hearts and minds, and we become renewed in truth.

Many times, these strongholds are the result of misunderstanding the finished work of the Cross and the righteousness we now possess before the throne of God. Again, when we pray in tongues, the spirit of revelation is touching our hearts and minds, and we are coming into truth. Stand strong today in what He's done and go to war!

TONGUES ACTIVATION PRAYER POINTS

- Thank Jesus for the work He completed on the Cross and in His resurrection.
- Thank Holy Spirit for the tools and strategies to exercise authority over your flesh and the devil.
- Ask Him to enable you to stand and fight the good fight of faith using those tools and strategies He has given you.

YOUR REFLECTIONS

YOUR REFLECTIONS

DAY TWO

PRAY IN THE SPIRIT AND PUT ON CHRIST

But put on the Lord Jesus Christ, and make no provision for the flesh, to fulfill its lusts.
—ROMANS 13:14 NKJV

There is one raging around this planet like a roaring lion, looking for those he can devour (see 1 Peter 5:8). In Romans 13, like many places in the New Testament, Paul calls us to "put on the Lord Jesus Christ." What exactly does that mean? I thought He was already on me. One of the most practical ways that I've found to obey this verse is through extended times of praying in tongues.

Over the past 20-plus years of regularly praying in tongues, I've found that around the 20-minute mark, my thoughts begin to change, my emotions begin to change, prayers start coming out of me, and I'm able to connect with God in an easier and more sustainable way. This is what I've come to understand "putting on the Lord Jesus Christ" to look like. It's stepping into the spirit, out of the soul. It's putting your spirit on the front seat of your bike and putting your soul on the back seat.

When we "put Him on" we are empowered and equipped to live, walk, talk, and fellowship in the Spirit. When "He comes on me," I feel His thoughts, His emotions, His prayers, His faith move through me.

Beloved, this is your inheritance—to be a conduit of the very life of Jesus Christ. Many believers live so below the poverty line of the Kingdom, and it's time for a generation to lay hold of the life of God residing within them. "Christ in you" is the answer to a thousand questions, circumstances, and difficulties. I dare you to set your heart, lift your eyes, and engage God by praying in tongues. Watch what happens!

TONGUES ACTIVATION PRAYER POINTS

- Thank Jesus for being in you.
- Ask Holy Spirit to empower you to put on Christ and make no provision for your flesh.
- Believe that, as you pray, ungodly desires and fleshly appetites completely lose their appeal to you.

YOUR REFLECTIONS

YOUR REFLECTIONS

DAY THREE

THE WARFARE OF INTIMACY

But I say, walk and live [habitually] in the [Holy] Spirit [responsive to and controlled and guided by the Spirit]; then you will certainly not gratify the cravings and desires of the flesh (of human nature without God).

—GALATIANS 5:16 AMPC

I cannot think of a clearer verse in the Bible that lays out the secret to an effective, victorious, and happy Christian life. Paul gives us an amazing law in the Kingdom. He in essence tells us that if we walk in the Spirit, we will not fulfill the lusts of the flesh. This is absolutely astounding. If we walk in the Spirit, then we will not look at pornography or be gripped with jealousy, anger, rage, fear, shame. The power of sin will be inoperative because we are living in a different realm called "the Spirit."

Yesterday, we looked at "putting on the Lord Jesus." Today, we are going to look at "walking in the Spirit." These two commands are the same command. They are the call to breakthrough out of our soul life and into our spirit life.

Many believers never experience the inexhaustible riches of God residing inside—and instead live defeated, anemic Christian lives. This is not what Jesus died for. He died that we would receive revelation of what we possess and then live a life of accessing this glory within.

How do you "walk in the Spirit"? The only way we will walk in the Spirit is by talking *to* the Spirit and talking *in* the Spirit. When we set our minds and hearts on the glory within and begin to draw on that life, His love, joy, peace, etc. will bubble up, changing the atmosphere in our minds, emotions, and bodies. Several verses later in Galatians 5:22-23 (NKJV), Paul tells us that the fruit of the Spirit, or the fruit of fellowshipping in the Spirit, is *"love, joy, peace, patience, kindness, goodness, faithfulness, gentleness, self-control."*

When we pray in tongues for extended periods of time, the fruit will be evident. This is the desire of God for every believer to live this life of manifesting the fruits of God. Every believer agrees that this is what God wants, but few of us practically know how to see this come about. Thanks be to God for the glorious gift of praying in tongues.

TONGUES ACTIVATION PRAYER POINTS

- Thank Holy Spirit for bearing fruit in your life.
- Tell Him that you're ready to stop striving and fighting in your own strength to become holy and walk in victory.
- Ask Him how to wage warfare from the position of intimacy.

YOUR REFLECTIONS

YOUR REFLECTIONS

DAY FOUR

YOUR OFFENSIVE WEAPONS

...the sword of the Spirit, which is the word of God. Pray in the Spirit at all times and on every occasion....

—EPHESIANS 6:17-18 NLT

After Paul lists the different parts of the armor of God for spiritual warfare in Ephesians 6:14-17, he concludes by sharing two offensive weapons. These two offensive weapons are the greatest and many times are the most underused weapons in the Christian life. They are the Word of God and praying in tongues for extended periods of time. These two weapons when put together are the greatest threats to the kingdom of darkness.

The Word of God is so powerful. The heavens were made through the Word of God. Nations have been built and destroyed by the Word. The sick have been healed, the demonized delivered, the dead raised by the Word of God, and this Word is living inside us and is right in front of us. However, when the Word of God is released through a mighty spirit, the force of the Word is felt.

When Jesus was in the wilderness being tempted by the devil, He fought the devil using the Word of God. When we build ourselves up through praying in the Spirit, the Word of God comes out of our spirits like a mighty sword cutting off the schemes of the evil one.

Many believers will live under oppression, sickness, fear, etc. and never open their mouths and declare the Word of God. We must do our part and release the Word of God through song and declaration. We must go from a defensive posture of just waiting for things to happen, to an offensive posture that builds a wall of fire around our lives and loved ones. I encourage you to take 25 minutes today to pray in the Spirit and declare the Word of God over those situations in your life that need breakthrough.

TONGUES ACTIVATION PRAYER POINTS

- Thank God for His Word and its power in your life.
- Ask Holy Spirit to quicken the Word of God in your spirit so that you can pray it back to Him.
- Ask Holy Spirit to move you beyond defensive warfare and into offensively releasing the Kingdom all around you.

YOUR REFLECTIONS

YOUR REFLECTIONS

DAY FIVE

WARFARE FROM VICTORY

Let the saints be joyful in glory; let them sing aloud on their beds. Let the high praises of God be in their mouth and a two-edged sword in their hand.
—PSALM 149:5-6 NKJV

This is one of those glorious passages that gives us a sneak peek of what the Church will look like in the generation of the Lord's return. We get to see in these verses the bringing together of joyful glory, singing the high praises of God from a place of rest, and at the same time the wielding of a double-edged sword, which is the Word of God.

As we spoke about at the beginning of this week, we don't fight from a place of trying to achieve victory, but from a place of already-received victory. Jesus won the victory 2,000 years ago at the Cross, and we get to partner with Him in the execution of the written sentence against the devil and his kingdom.

We are seated with Christ in heavenly places; and as we sing in the Spirit and as we sing the Word of God, He binds, He destroys, He delivers us from our enemies. What the devil attempted to get when he tried to usurp God's throne, God has freely given us through the death and resurrection of Jesus.

On this last day of the week, I want you to take a deep breath, fill your mind with thoughts of where you are now in the heavenly places, and begin to sing in the Spirit straight to the throne. As you do this, know that the atmosphere around you is being changed and that your enemies are being destroyed. Just as Jehoshaphat put the singers ahead of the army and God routed out their enemies, so God is raising up a people who will sing from a place of rest and watch God fight our battles for us.

TONGUES ACTIVATION PRAYER POINTS

- Sing a song of thanksgiving for the victory Jesus already accomplished for you.
- Ask Holy Spirit to empower you to enforce Jesus's victory in every situation from a place of rest.
- Ask Holy Spirit to fight for you.

YOUR REFLECTIONS

YOUR REFLECTIONS

Week Eight

How to Activate the Power of Holy Spirit in Your Life

Day One

THERE IS MORE AVAILABLE FOR YOU

And I will pray the Father, and He will give you another Helper, that He may abide with you forever.
—John 14:16 NKJV

...but tarry in the city of Jerusalem until you are endued with power from on high.
—Luke 24:49 NKJV

There is so much more! I'm so grateful for the gift of salvation and all that it entails. I'm so grateful for the life of the Spirit within me. I'm so grateful for the gift of tongues and all the glorious benefits that have come into my life because of giving myself to it for years. In light of all of this, I want you to know there is more. Whether the "more" is something that comes from above or breaks out from within, I don't really care. I just know there is more.

Jesus, in a resurrected body, spent 40 days with 500 people, teaching on the Kingdom of God, and still that wasn't enough for them to begin Christianity. Out of 500, 380 of them thought that it was enough because only 120 made it to the upper room, obeying Jesus's command to "wait for the promise of the Spirit." Throughout the book of Acts and throughout history, we see that there are ongoing, fresh baptisms of the Holy Spirit for greater witness and power on earth. This is what I'm desperate for, and my prayer is that you would become hungry for the same reality in your life.

I'm sad to say that so many "Spirit-filled" believers have turned their prayer language into a badge of having arrived into the fullness of God and have stopped reaching in their spiritual life for the fullness of God.

In Ephesians 5, Paul commands us to go on being filled with Holy Spirit. His understanding is that it's not a one-time experience but an ever-increasing encounter with the Person who is bringing you into greater realms of intimacy and power.

I believe that if we steward the gift of tongues, then God will open us up to greater gifts as well as greater realms of intimacy and power with Himself.

This last week is about giving you a vision for the rest of your days here on earth of full immersion into God Himself. Begin to ask God to make you hungry for more. He loves to answer!

TONGUES ACTIVATION PRAYER POINTS

- Thank Holy Spirit for enduing you "with power from on high."

- Ask Him to make you hungry and desperate for more of Him, more of His filling, and more of His power, so that your life can be an even greater witness for Him.
- Ask Him to increase your capacity for more of Him.

YOUR REFLECTIONS

YOUR REFLECTIONS

DAY TWO

HE'S A GOOD FATHER

...how much more will your heavenly Father give the Holy Spirit to those who ask Him!
—LUKE 11:13 NKJV

When it comes to receiving fresh baptisms and immersions in the life and power of Holy Spirit, you must understand that the Person you are asking is the kindest, most generous, most powerful Person you will ever meet. In Luke 11, Jesus gives us great confidence when asking God to fill us with Holy Spirit by letting us know that, if we ask Him for bread, He will not give us a stone, but will give us the very thing that we are asking for.

The second thing Jesus lets us know is that compared to God, we are all evil. No matter how good you think you are, all of us are evil compared to Father. Jesus said that if we, being evil, have the capacity to give good gifts to our own children, how much more will our heavenly Father give good gifts to His children?

God is not the kind of father who makes you go outside and work for eight hours before you can open your Christmas gifts, nor is He the kind of father who keeps hiding from you so that you can never find him. God the Father draws us out through promises to ask Him; and it's when we ask, seek, and knock that doors open. He is the good Father who is brilliant in His leadership in bringing us the fullness of His plan. He is gracious, compassionate, merciful, all-powerful, all wise, all-knowing, and He loves to give good gifts.

TONGUES ACTIVATION PRAYER POINTS

- Thank God for being the good Father who answers your prayers and requests.
- Ask Holy Spirit to unveil the heart and nature of the Father.
- Ask Him to awaken faith in you to trust more and more in the faithfulness of God to answer your prayers.

YOUR REFLECTIONS

YOUR REFLECTIONS

DAY THREE

THE KEY OF HUNGER

Blessed are you who hunger now, for you shall be filled....
—LUKE 6:21 NKJV

In His Sermon on the Mount, Jesus gave us the true definition of success and happiness in God's eyes. He spoke specifically about cultivating eight realities in our lives that God deems as "blessed." Among these is the blessing of hungering for righteousness. Hunger is the currency to the Kingdom. The whole Kingdom is accessed through hunger.

If there is one principle that the gospel makes clear, it is this: Jesus simply does things for hungry people that He doesn't do for everyone else. The woman with the issue of blood, the Canaanite woman, and Blind Bartimaeus are all stories of people who pressed past all opposition and all fear to lay hold of Jesus and receive what they sought.

Paul himself declares in Philippians 3:12 (NKJV), *"Not that I have already attained, or am already perfected; but I press on, that I may lay hold of that for which Christ Jesus has also laid hold of me.*" You need to ask yourself this question: Why did Jesus lay hold of your life and save you? Paul's whole life was a violent, hungry search to discover the answer to that question.

One of my heroes in the faith in modern times is John G. Lake. There are many aspects of his life that are admirable, but the greatest one to me was a high vision for the life of God in man, which thereby released an amazing hunger in this man's life. To him, greater intimacy with Jesus and power were one and the same thing. His longing was for greater nearness to God, which released greater realms of power, but his desire was greater proximity to Jesus.

I have a question for you: Are you hungry for God? Honestly, are you hungry? Hunger is when a desire becomes the ultimate obsession in your life; and until it is answered, you will not be satisfied. Let us pray to get hungry.

TONGUES ACTIVATION PRAYER POINTS

- Thank God for seasons of hunger in your life.
- Ask Holy Spirit to increase your hunger for greater intimacy with Jesus.
- Ask Him for the blessing that comes with hunger—the satisfaction of greater proximity and intimacy with Him.

YOUR REFLECTIONS

YOUR REFLECTIONS

DAY FOUR

JESUS THE BAPTIST

...He will baptize you with the Holy Spirit and fire.
—MATTHEW 3:11 NKJV

I believe God wants to fill you afresh today with His fire and glory and change your life. Today, we cast off all our badges and former experiences and simply ask God to fill us with His Holy Spirit. He is the good Father, and He loves to give good gifts to His children. If you ask Him, He will answer you with the very thing you are desiring. You can never be good enough to receive it or work hard enough to earn it because it's a free gift. All you need to do is simply ask, open your heart, and receive. When you feel Him rising up within you, open your mouth and pray in Holy Spirit.

John the Baptist's favorite title for Jesus was *Jesus the Baptist*. In each of the four Gospels, John points to One who would come and provide a baptism that was far beyond what people were experiencing in water. He continually declared that there was One coming who would baptize you with Holy Spirit and fire.

One of the primary missions of Jesus was to come, die, be raised again, ascend, and baptize the Church with Holy Spirit and fire. This mission will become very clear in the coming days as we move into the greatest hour ever.

Today, let's ask for a fresh baptism—immersion into Holy Spirit. Open your heart and ask God for it. He will meet you.

TONGUES ACTIVATION PRAYER POINTS

- Thank Jesus for paying for your sin on the Cross, granting you eternal life and giving you Holy Spirit here on earth as a down payment.
- Ask Father to baptize you afresh in Holy Spirit's power and presence—to fill you to overflowing.
- Ask Holy Spirit to grow you in character and in power to operate in all His gifts for the glory of God the Father.

YOUR REFLECTIONS

YOUR REFLECTIONS

DAY FIVE

THE SPIRIT AND THE BRIDE SAY, "COME!"

And the Spirit and the bride say, "Come!" And let him who hears say, "Come!" And let him who thirsts come. Whoever desires, let him take the water of life freely.
—REVELATION 22:17 NKJV

In Revelation 22:17, we see an amazing prophecy of what the Church will look like before the coming of the Lord. This verse contains three specific realities that will be manifested on earth.

The first thing is that there is coming a day when Holy Spirit and the Church will come into unity with each other. God will release great glory and crisis in the earth for the purpose of joining His Church with the agenda of Holy Spirit. He will shake everything that can be shaken so that we will awaken to everything He died for. For the past 2,000 years, the Church has been on AM (to use radio language), and Holy Spirit has been on FM, but there is coming a day when the very desires of Holy Spirit will become the desires of the Church.

As the Church and Holy Spirit come into unity with one another, Holy Spirit will begin to shift the identity of the Church into a new identity and give us a new name—the bride. Holy Spirit is emphasizing Jesus as the Bridegroom God, which will thereby change the way we see ourselves. This bride will love what He loves and hate what He hates. She will be in full agreement with His will and purpose and will partner with Him in bringing His Kingdom to earth.

This bride will partner with the Bridegroom in the primary anointing that He is releasing on the end-time Church—prayer. It will be the prayer, "Come," that will call Jesus back to the planet, rapture the saints, judge the wicked, and save the nation of Israel.

How does all of this relate to tongues? I'm glad you asked! As we give ourselves to years and even decades of praying in the Spirit, we are brought into unity with His mind, will, and purpose, our identities are changed into bridal identity, and the anointing of prayer comes on our lives with an increasing understanding of the end-time drama.

Holy Spirit is awakening the Church all around the earth from her slumber, and it will be through praying in tongues that the Church will come into her greatest hour.

TONGUES ACTIVATION PRAYER POINTS

- Thank Holy Spirit for leading you through these weeks of praying in tongues.
- Ask Him to continue leading you on this great journey with Him, partnering with

Him to see awakening in your life and in the world.

- Ask Jesus to make you and the rest of His bride ready for His return—just ask Him to "Come, Lord Jesus."

YOUR REFLECTIONS

YOUR REFLECTIONS

ABOUT COREY RUSSELL

Corey Russell's passion is to awaken the Church across the earth to the revelation of Jesus, intimacy with Holy Spirit, and the power of prayer.

He has written 9 books, released 6 prayer albums, and is discipling many through his online school at coreyrussellonline.com. He is currently on the pastoral team at House Denver. He lives in Denver, Colorado, with his family.

Made in the USA
Columbia, SC
26 September 2024